INTERACT ™

THE BOOK AN[...] [...]K TOGETHER

T0124098

REPTILES

TWO CAN ™

CHANHASSEN, MINNESOTA · LONDON

Copyright © 2004 Two-Can Publishing

Two-Can Publishing
An imprint of Creative Publishing international, Inc.
18705 Lake Drive East
Chanhassen, MN 55317
1-800-328-3895
www.two-canpublishing.com

Created by
John Brown Junior
The New Boathouse
136-142 Bramley Road
London W10 6SR

Project Manager: Deborah Kespert
Art Director: Belinda Webster
Senior Designer: Liz Adcock
Editor: Paul Virr
Author: Susie Brooks
Illustrator: Simone End
Consultant: Michael Chinery

ISBN 1-58728-417-0

Library of Congress Cataloging-in-Publication Data: pending

Photographic credits: Cover Naturepl.com/Kevin Schafer; 8-9 Getty Images/Image Bank/Guido Alberto Rossi; 11t NHPA/James Carmichael Jr.; 11b NHPA/James Carmichael Jr.; 12 Ardea/Adrian Warren; 13 NHPA/James Carmichael Jr.; 14 Naturepl.com/Peter Oxford; 15 Ardea/Ian Beams; 16 Ardea/M. Watson; 17 Ardea/Valerie Taylor; 18 OSF/David Thompson; 19 Getty Images/Image Bank/Steven Hunt; 21 Corbis/Jeffrey L. Rotman; 22t NHPA/Rich Kirchner; 22b OSF/Terry Button; 23 NHPA/David Heuclin; 24-5 Naturepl.com/Neil P. Lucas; 25 Corbis/Stuart Westmoreland; 26 NHPA/Norbert Wu; 27 OSF/Michael Fogden; 28 Corbis/Gallo Images/Anthony Bannister; 30 NHPA/Daniel Heuclin; 31 OSF/Belinda Wright

1 2 3 4 5 6 09 08 07 06 05 04

Printed in China

INTERFACT ™

INTERFACT will have you hooked in minutes – and that's a fact!

The disk is packed with interactive puzzles, quizzes, and videos. You'll find in-depth facts and links to some great reptile web sites.

▶ Play CHANGING PLACES. Rearrange the tiles to find the lizards.

VOICE OFF

Click to continue

Change feature

Open the book and discover more fascinating information, highlighted with colorful illustrations and photographs.

Crocodiles and alligators

Crocodiles and alligators are members of a group of reptiles called crocodilians. You can recognize them by their long, snapping jaws, their broad, low-slung body and their powerful, whipping tail. Crocodilians live in tropical areas and spend most of their time in water, although they are also at home on land. They are covered with thick scales, and they have bony scales along their back that act as a protective armour.

Most crocodiles are large, fierce predators. Their jaws are lined with pointed teeth that can kill small prey with a single bite. A male crocodile warns other crocodiles and animals to keep away from its food and territory by slapping its head down loudly on the water with a snap of its jaws. Crocodiles and alligators also roar like lions, and communicate using smells, body movements and underwater vibrations.

SPOT THE DIFFERENCE

Crocodiles and alligators look similar, but not identical. Here's how to tell them apart.

alligator

crocodile

When the mouth is closed, the upper jaw hides most of the lower teeth, including the long fourth tooth.

When the jaws are closed, both upper and lower teeth are visible and the fourth lower tooth sits outside the jaw.

The alligator has a wide head and jaw, with a U-shaped snout.

The crocodile has a narrow head and jaw, with a V-shaped snout.

DISK LINK
Play SNAP ATTACK and answer questions about reptiles to save the alligator from an alligator ambush!

◀ Find out all about crocodiles and their relative s alligators, gharials, and caimans.

To make the most of INTERFACT, use the book and disk together. Look out for special signs called Disk Links and Bookmarks. To find out more, turn to page 43.

40

BOOKMARK

DISK LINK
Play CHANGING PLACES and complete the two picture puzzles to see lizards in action.

DISK LINK

Once you've clicked on to INTERFACT, you'll never look back.

LOAD UP!
Go to **page 41** to find out how to load your disk and click into action.

What's on the Disk?

Help Screen

Learn how to use your Interfact disk in no time at all. Use the voice button to switch the sound on or off. Use your arrow keys to select a game or bring up the Help icon.

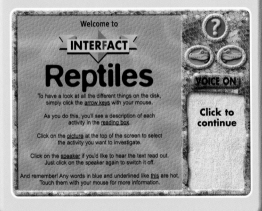

Welcome to

INTERFACT

Reptiles

To have a look at all the different things on the disk, simply click the arrow keys with your mouse.

As you do this, you'll see a description of each activity in the reading box.

Click on the picture at the top of the screen to select the activity you want to investigate.

Click on the speaker if you'd like to hear the text read out. Just click on the speaker again to switch it off.

And remember! Any words in blue and underlined like this are hot. Touch them with your mouse for more information.

VOICE ON

Click to continue

A crocodile sometimes swallows stones to help it break down its food.

TRUE   FALSE

Snap Attack

Answer ten questions about reptiles correctly, and you'll be high and dry in the Everglades. But linger too long and you could be on the menu!

Snake Escape

Can you help the sea snake outwit the hungry shark? You'll have to spell out the name of a mystery reptile. It could be anything from a Komodo dragon to a caiman. Guess a letter and type it on your keyboard to see if you're right. Don't worry if you get stuck. All the mystery reptiles are named in the book.

K_m_d_ d_ag_n

LETTERS USED
e f t s i
b h

Changing Places

Rearrange the tiles to see if you can solve the picture puzzles. There are two brain-teasers to tackle and two lizards to discover. If you can unscramble all the squares, you're in for a dazzling display!

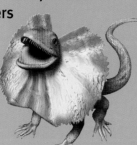

Shuffle   Change picture

Movie Theater

Sit back, relax, and enjoy video clips of reptiles in action. Watch a chameleon catch an insect to eat, join a green turtle for a swim in the tropical sea, and take cover as a rattlesnake strikes!

Turtle swimming over reef

Chameleon

Turtle

Rattlesnake

This green turtle is swimming over a coral reef. It beats its flippers in the same way that a bird flaps its wings. A remora fish hitches a ride, attaching itself with a special sucker on its head.

Net Notebook

Take a look at these links to great reptile web sites. You'll find a sneak preview and a description of each one to help you choose. There's a lot to discover about reptiles on the Internet!

National Geographic.com Kids – Creature Feature: Nile Crocodiles

This special area of the National Geographic Kids site is dedicated to the Nile crocodile. Click on the "Fun Facts" button, and you'll find a scrolling list of facts about their life span, habitat, history, diet, behavior, and much more. There's also a world map showing where in Africa the Nile crocodile lives.

http://www.nationalgeographic.com/kids/creature_feature/0107/crocodiles.html

What's in the Book?

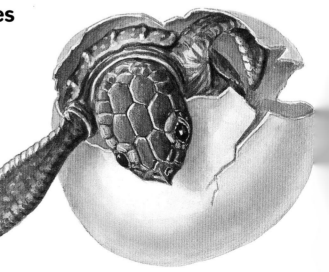

Many of the reptiles in this book are featured on the disk.

*All words in the text that appear in **bold** can be found in the glossary.*

What Is a Reptile?

Reptiles come in many shapes and sizes. They include darting lizards, slow-moving tortoises, graceful sea turtles, fierce crocodiles, and slithering snakes.

Reptiles are **vertebrates**, which means they have a backbone. Most reptiles have four legs, but some, such as snakes, have no legs at all. You can recognize a reptile by its dry, scaly skin, which keeps in body moisture and provides a waterproof coat.

Reptiles are **cold-blooded**. This means their bodies are as hot or cold as the air around them. They need be warm to be active, so sometimes reptiles have to sunbathe before they can move around much. Most reptiles live on land, but some, such as crocodiles, live in water. The majority of reptiles lay eggs.

▼ Marine iguanas are a type of lizard. They live on the Gálapagos Islands in the Pacific Ocean.

DID YOU KNOW?

● There are nearly 6,000 **species** of reptile alive today.

The first reptiles lived more than 300 million years ago. Dinosaurs were types of reptile that have died out.

People who study reptiles are called **herpetologists**.

A REPTILE'S BODY

Many reptiles, like this chameleon, have long, low-slung bodies, long tails, and short legs that stick out from the sides of their bodies. The chameleon also has some unique features of its own.

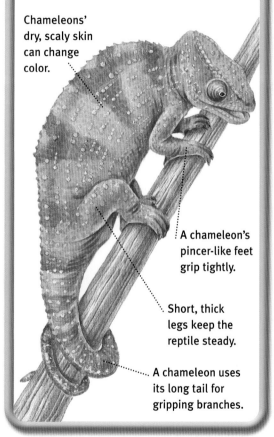

Chameleons' dry, scaly skin can change color.

A chameleon's pincer-like feet grip tightly.

Short, thick legs keep the reptile steady.

A chameleon uses its long tail for gripping branches.

VIDEO CLIP LINK

Check out the video clips on the disk to see how a chameleon uses its long tongue to catch prey.

Where Reptiles Live

Reptiles are found in most regions of the world, except for extremely cold areas, such as the North and South **Poles**. They live in all kinds of places, from scorching, dry deserts and steamy **rain forests** to vast oceans and murky **swamps**.

Many reptiles live in parts of the world with a warm **climate**. This allows them to be active all year long, even though they are cold-blooded. Other reptiles live in cooler areas. When winter arrives, they save energy by going into a deep sleep called **hibernation**. They sleep through the cold months until warmer weather returns.

▼ This map shows where six particular reptile species are found. Reptiles live on all of the continents except Antarctica.

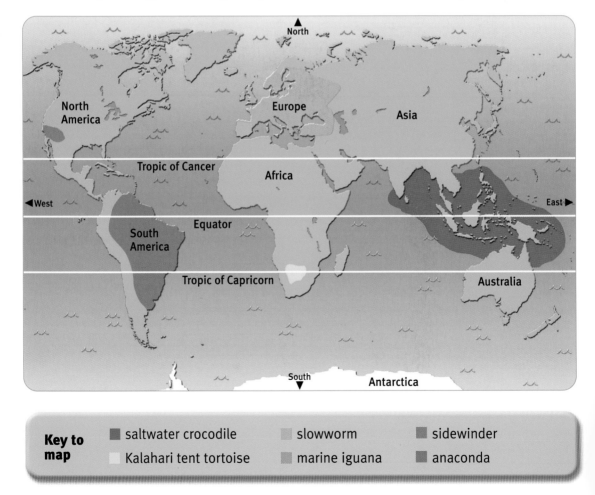

North

North America

Europe

Asia

Tropic of Cancer

Africa

◄ West

East ▶

Equator

South America

Tropic of Capricorn

Australia

South

Antarctica

Key to map	■ saltwater crocodile	■ slowworm	■ sidewinder
	■ Kalahari tent tortoise	■ marine iguana	■ anaconda

◄ The Gila monster is a lizard that lives in the deserts of Mexico and the United States. Food is often scarce, so it can survive for a long time on fat stored in its tail.

▼ Tropical rain forests are home to the widest variety of reptiles. This Amazon tree boa uses its scales to grip as it coils around a branch.

Lizards

Lizards usually have a large head with two bulging eyes, a narrow body, four short legs, claws, and a long, pointed tail. Some species have a crest on their back or a frill around their neck. Lizards vary in color from dull brown to bright red and green. The chameleon can even change its color according to its mood or surroundings!

There are about 3,500 lizard species, more than any other kind of reptile. They range from tiny geckos to giant Komodo dragons, and from quick chameleons to slow, deadly Gila monsters. Lizards are easy to spot because they hunt for their **prey** during the day. Most lizards are **carnivores**, or meat eaters, feeding on insects, birds, and other small animals.

▶ Geckos are expert climbers. They have widely spaced toes, and the soles of their feet have tiny, sucker-tipped hairs on them. These hairs allow geckos to cling to almost any surface, even when they're upside down!

▼ The Komodo dragon of Indonesia is the world's largest lizard. It can grow to more than 10 feet (3 m) long, which is the length of a small car! The Komodo usually feeds on **carrion**, but it can kill its own dinner, too!

DISK LINK
Play CHANGING PLACES and complete the two picture puzzles to see lizards in action.

DID YOU KNOW?

● A few lizards, such as the slowworm and some skinks, have no legs at all.

● Only two species of lizard are **venomous**, injecting poison into their victims. These are the Mexican beaded lizard and the Gila monster.

● A gecko can't blink, so it cleans its eyes with its long tongue.

Snakes

Snakes are closely related to lizards. There are more than 2,300 species of snake in the world, and they live both on land and in water. Rain forests are home to the widest variety of snakes, but these slithering reptiles also inhabit deserts, mountains, grasslands, forests, and oceans.

Snakes have long, flexible bodies with no limbs. The use their strong muscles to push themselves forward. Their smooth, scaly skin stretches slightly, allowing them to slither along.

Most snakes feed on small creatures such as insects, mice, and frogs. They are expert hunters, but they cannot hear well and their eyesight is poor. Some snakes use **heat sensors** to detect their prey, while others sense **vibrations** around them. Many snakes "taste" the air with their darting tongues.

Some snake species kill their prey with venom. Others suffocate their victims by squeezing them until they can't breathe. This is called **constriction**. A powerful anaconda can squeeze a crocodile to death!

FINDING FOOD

Snakes "taste" the air with their tongue to detect when dinner is nearby.

Snakes have nostrils but these are not very sensitive.

A notch in the upper lip allows the tongue to shoot in and out, even when the mouth is closed.

A forked tongue helps the snake to figure out where a smell is coming from.

A sensor in the roof of the mouth called the Jacobson's organ identifies the smell sensed by the tongue.

◀ This viper has long, hinged fangs that fold back into its mouth when they're not needed. When the snake attacks, the fangs spring forward to strike the prey. At the same time, they squirt out a jet of venom that **paralyzes** the victim and keeps it from fighting back. The viper is then ready to enjoy its meal. Like all snakes, it swallows its food whole with a series of large, slow gulps and **digests** it over several days.

▶ This Pope's pit viper is **sloughing**, or shedding, its skin. A snake's skin doesn't grow with its body, so two or three times a year, the snake replaces it. Starting at the head, it rubs off the tough outer layer in one piece, to reveal a brand-new layer of shiny skin underneath. The snake then slithers away, leaving its old skin behind in a dry, shriveled heap.

Harmless or Deadly?

Venomous snakes include cobras, mambas, and vipers. They all have fangs that inject venom into their prey. Sometimes a bite is enough to kill an animal, but more often the venom paralyzes the victim or slowly starts to break down its blood and muscles.

Not all snakes are venomous. Grass snakes, for example, have a harmless bite. Sometimes it's difficult to tell venomous and nonvenomous snakes apart. The harmless milk snake has markings similar to the dangerous coral snake. It only pretends to be venomous to keep enemies away!

▶ The king cobra is the world's largest venomous snake. It can grow to 20 feet (6 m) in length. Its head is as large as a man's hand. An angry cobra rears up and makes itself bigger by stretching the skin and ribs of its neck into a huge hood. This warns enemies that the snake is ready to strike.

DID YOU KNOW?

● Only one in ten types of snake has venom that is dangerous to humans, and only a few of these can kill.

● The black mamba is one of the most feared snakes. It is intelligent, aggressive, venomous, and very fast.

● Flying snakes can flatten their bodies and glide from tree to tree!

Constrictors

Snakes that squeeze their prey to death are known as constrictors. They include boas, which live mainly in South America, and pythons, which live in Africa and Southeast Asia. There are many different species of boa and python, and among them are the world's largest snakes. Constrictors are not venomous. They attack their prey in two stages: first they grab it and grip it with their sharp teeth; then they wrap themselves tightly around the victim and squeeze until it suffocates. After that, they swallow it whole.

Water Snakes

Some snakes live in water. There are about 50 different kinds of snake that live in the sea. All sea snakes are highly venomous, but they aren't aggressive, and they hardly ever attack humans.

About 30 different kinds of snake live in rivers, streams, and swamps. These freshwater snakes are not venomous, but some of them are constrictors.

Water snakes occasionally come to land to bask in the sun, but they spend most of their time in water. Their nostrils are on top of their heads, so they can breathe while their bodies remain underwater.

Water snakes have strong tail muscles and are powerful swimmers. They can move fast enough to catch fish and frogs.

DISK LINK
Play SNAKE ESCAPE and guess reptile words to help the sea snake escape from the shark.

▶ Sea snakes, such as this banded sea snake, spend their whole life at sea. Unlike other snakes, their young are born right in the water. They have flat tails that work like paddles. And flaps cover their nostrils to keep the water out. Sea snakes kill fish with their venom. **Predators** of this snake even need to beware. If a creature swallows a sea snake whole, the snake can bite its stomach from the inside! The yellow-bellied sea snake has the deadliest venom of any snake.

Tortoises and Turtles

There are about 200 species of turtles, tortoises, and their relatives, terrapins. They all have one thing in common—a tough shell. This shell is domed on top and flat on the bottom. It is made up of bony plates that are joined together and covered with giant scales called **scutes**.

Except for sea turtles, each reptile in this group can pull its head, legs, and tail inside its shell to protect itself from predators. Then it simply waits until the danger has passed before coming out.

The main difference between turtles and tortoises is their **habitat**. Turtles live in the water, or partly on land and partly in water. Sea turtles spend most of their lives at sea, but they return to land to lay eggs. They even have flippers to help them swim. Tortoises, however, live on land and don't swim.

▶ To help a green sea turtle swim, its shell is lighter in weight and more streamlined than a tortoise's. Turtles swim underwater, but most surface for air every few minutes.

STRUCTURE OF A TORTOISE SHELL

The upper part of the shell is called the carapace.

The backbone and ribs are fused to the carapace.

The lower part of the shell is called the plastron.

The scutes are made from a tough, horn-like material.

▲ Tortoises are the slowest-moving reptiles, but this Kalahari tent tortoise doesn't need to run away from its enemies. Its shell is **camouflaged** to help the tortoise blend in with its desert home. It is nearly impossible for a predator to get the tortoise out.

VIDEO CLIP LINK
Check out the video clips
on the disk and watch a
green sea turtle swimming
over a coral reef.

Crocodiles and Alligators

Crocodiles and alligators are members of a group of reptiles called crocodilians. You can recognize them by their long, snapping jaws, their broad, low-slung bodies, and their powerful, whip-like tails. Crocodilians live in **tropical** areas and spend most of their time in water, although they are also at home on land. They are covered with thick scales, and they have bony scutes along their backs that act as protective armor.

Most crocodilians are large, fierce predators. Their jaws are lined with pointed teeth that can kill small prey with a single bite. A male crocodile warns other crocodiles and animals to keep away from its food and **territory** by slapping its head down loudly on the water with a snap of its jaws. Crocodiles and alligators also roar like lions and communicate using smells, body movements, and underwater vibrations.

SPOT THE DIFFERENCE

Alligators and crocodiles look similar, but not identical. Here's how to tell them apart.

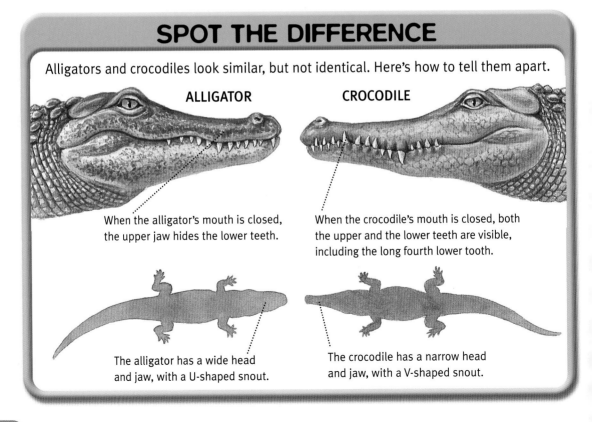

ALLIGATOR

CROCODILE

When the alligator's mouth is closed, the upper jaw hides the lower teeth.

When the crocodile's mouth is closed, both the upper and the lower teeth are visible, including the long fourth lower tooth.

The alligator has a wide head and jaw, with a U-shaped snout.

The crocodile has a narrow head and jaw, with a V-shaped snout.

▶ A crocodile can use its tail like a propeller to launch itself out of the water. This saltwater crocodile is "tail-walking," hoping to catch a low-flying bird to eat for dinner.

DISK LINK
Play SNAP ATTACK and answer questions about reptiles to save the ranger from an alligator ambush!

▲ This alligator may look as if it's yawning, but in fact it's trying to cool down. In hot weather, crocodiles and alligators keep their temperature down by opening their jaws. This exposes the moist skin inside the mouth to the air. As the moisture evaporates in the heat, it cools down the animal.

▶ A crocodile's eyes, ears, and nostrils are located on top of its head, so it can lie almost completely underwater. Sometimes a crocodile swallows stones to help it digest its food, and this may help weigh down its body. Hiding underwater is great for launching a surprise attack. The crocodile lurks there without moving, waiting for its prey to pass by. A well-timed leap is all it takes to grab an easy meal.

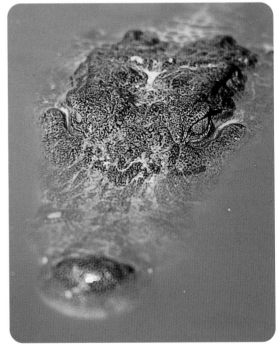

Caimans and Gharials

The crocodilian family also includes caimans, found in Central and South America, and gharials, from northern India. Both of these animals look similar to crocodiles and alligators, but it's easy to tell them apart. Caimans are smaller than their relatives, and they move more quickly on land. They have short snouts and long teeth. Gharials are one of the largest crocodilian species, with long, narrow jaws. Their feet are strongly webbed and ideal for swimming.

▼ A gharial's jaws are perfect for catching fish, its favorite food. The gharial swims with its mouth wide open until a fish slips inside. Then the jaws slam shut and spear it with rows of spiky teeth.

DID YOU KNOW?

● Of the 23 crocodilian species, two types are considered to be man-eaters—the saltwater crocodile, from Southeast Asia and northern Australia, and Africa's Nile crocodile.

● Most crocodilians live in fresh water. Only the saltwater crocodile, or "salty," can live in sea water. Its body is able to rid itself of excess salt.

● Some crocodilians can live for up to 100 years. Crocodiles usually live longer than alligators.

On the Move

Reptiles get around in many different ways. They crawl, scuttle, wriggle, swim, climb, burrow, or even glide. Some reptiles are fast and agile, while others are slow and sturdy. Each has a body shape that has **adapted** over many generations to suit its particular habitat.

Small lizards are quick on their feet so that they can escape from predators. Their narrow bodies are built for running and climbing. A few tree lizards, such as the flying gecko, can even glide through the air. They have flaps of skin on their legs that work like parachutes to help them "fly" from branch to branch.

Crocodiles and alligators are powerful swimmers. They push themselves through the water by swishing their tails from side to side and steering with their webbed back feet.

The basilisk lizard, from South America, runs upright on its back legs. If it gets up enough speed, it can even run across the surface of water for short distances!

Even though they have no legs, some snakes can move just as fast as a person can walk. Most snakes wriggle using an s-shaped motion, while a few crawl like caterpillars. Many snakes can climb trees, using their scales to grip the bark.

► Tortoises have heavy shells, so they can't move very fast. The largest species is the Galápagos giant tortoise, which can weigh over 500 pounds (225 kg). It takes this huge tortoise about 2 seconds to make one step, or about 6½ hours to travel 1 mile (1.6 km)! Turtles have lighter shells than tortoises, but they are still clumsy on land. They are more graceful in the water. Sea turtles can swim at speeds of up to 16 miles per hour (25 kph).

▼ The sidewinder rattlesnake of the United States curls into an S-shape, then flings itself sideways across the hot, slippery sand. Only two parts of its body touch the ground at one time, so it does not scorch its skin. This motion leaves distinctive tracks in the sand.

F eding Tim

Most reptiles are carnivores, hunting regularly for other animals to eat. But they can survive without food for long periods of time. This is because they are cold-blooded, which means they rely on the sun, not energy from food, to keep them warm. They can also survive with little to drink. Their thick, waterproof skin keeps them from drying out.

Tortoises feed on plants. They are too slow to catch other animals. Some turtles will eat plants, but most prefer fish, insects, frogs, crabs, and snakes.

Crocodiles and alligators like their meals to be big. They attack large animals, such as deer, zebra, and buffalo. They drag their prey underwater to drown, and then eat them.

▲ A snake can unhook its jaws when it eats, allowing it to swallow food that's much larger than its own head. This South African egg-eater snake is feasting on a bird's egg. The snake has tooth-like spines in its throat that crack open the shell, releasing the yolk. It then spits out the shell in one mushy lump.

◄ Most lizards stick to a diet of insects, such as flies, beetles, grasshoppers, and ants. This three-horned chameleon is about to capture a snack. A chameleon's tongue has a sticky lump at the end that latches onto the insect. The tongue is as long as the chameleon's body, and it can shoot out in a split second to take a victim by surprise.

DID YOU KNOW?

● Reptiles' jaws are not made for chewing—they can only tear their food or swallow it whole.

● Some birds hop into crocodiles' mouths to pick scraps from between their teeth! The bird gets a meal, and the crocodile gets its teeth cleaned.

● Some large pythons can go for a whole year without eating anything. Crocodiles need to eat only about once a week.

Reptile Babies

Like most animals, reptiles mate to produce their young. Most lay eggs or give birth to live young on land—even sea turtles, who spend most of their lives in water.

Most reptile species hatch from eggs. The shells are leathery and waterproof, making them tougher than the thin, brittle shells of birds' eggs. Reptiles usually lay several eggs at a time. A few reptiles, such as the horned lizard, give birth to live young.

Reptile babies usually look like their parents. The young of many reptile species look after themselves, because the mothers leave their eggs to hatch on their own.

A few types of reptile stay to care for their young after they are born. Alligators and crocodiles carry their newly hatched young to the water and look after them for many weeks. Pythons are the only snakes that stay with their eggs until they hatch.

DID YOU KNOW?

Reptiles that lay eggs are called **oviparous**. Reptiles that produce live young are **viviparous** and usually live in cooler climates.

A sea turtle can lay as many as 200 eggs at a time, and up to 800 in one season! Very few of the **hatchlings** will survive to adulthood.

Baby crocodiles let their mother know when they're ready to hatch by making a high-pitched noise. When the mother hears them, she digs up the buried eggs, and the young hatch.

▶ A baby snake has a sharp ridge of skin called an egg tooth on the top of its snout. The egg tooth is hard to see, but it is quite useful for breaking through a tough eggshell.

Journey of Life

Every two to four years, an adult female leatherback sea turtle swims back to the stretch of coastline where she was born to lay her eggs. She may swim more than 3,000 miles (5,000 km) across the ocean.

1 ▲ Turtles **migrate** from feeding grounds to breeding grounds, areas of the ocean where they gather to mate.

2 ▼ The female turtle crawls ashore at night to dig a nest. She lays her eggs, buries them, and returns to the sea.

3 ▲ About 60 days later, hatching begins. The baby turtles dig their way out of the nest.

4 ◄ The hatchlings race for the sea, guided by moonlight on the water. Many are eaten by predators on the way.

eptile Def nses

Reptiles have developed many ways to protect themselves from enemies. Hiding, running, and fighting are some of the skills they use to stay safe.

Keeping out of sight is easy if you blend in with your surroundings. Many reptiles' skin colors and patterns are designed for camouflage. The leaf-tailed gecko is a good example of this. It blends in with tree bark so well that predators don't notice it.

Some reptiles run rather than hide. Glass snakes and many lizards can perform an amazing trick. If one of them is caught by its tail, the tail snaps off so that the reptile can run away. The tail soon grows back.

Other reptiles scare away attackers by surprising them in some way. The desert horned lizard can squirt blood from its eyes!

▶ The Australian frilled lizard defends itself by opening a fan-like collar. This makes the lizard look much bigger than it really is.

▼ Snakes hiss when they're alarmed, but the rattlesnake does even better. It flicks the end of its tail to make a loud rattling noise.

VIDEO CLIP LINK
Check out the video clips to see what happens when a western diamondback rattlesnake strikes!

Reptile Record-Breakers

You've seen how many different kinds of reptile there are and how varied their lives can be, but you might be surprised by some of these scaly statistics. For instance, did you know that tortoises are the longest-living of all reptiles? They can live for more than 150 years. And the most ancient species of reptile alive today is the tuatara. This rare, lizard-like reptile makes its home in New Zealand. It has changed little since the time of the dinosaurs. That's why it is sometimes called a "living fossil."

▶ **Smallest Reptile**
The world's smallest reptile is probably the dwarf gecko, which measures .6 inches (16 mm) long. That's just over half an inch! It's so tiny, it can fit on an adult human's thumb. The British Virgin Islands gecko takes second place at .7 inches (18 mm) long.

▼ **Longest Reptile**
Female reticulated pythons of Southeast Asia and Indonesia can grow to more than 33 feet (10 m) long. A full-grown adult can swallow a large deer—including the antlers!

▼ Most Massive Reptile

The saltwater crocodile of Southeast Asia and Australia can grow to over 20 feet (6 m) long and can weigh more than 2,200 pounds (1 t). These huge beasts lurk by the water's edge, waiting for their prey. They feed on wild dogs, cattle, other crocodiles, and sometimes humans.

▼ Fastest Reptile

The Costa Rican spiny-tailed iguana is a fast sprinter. It has been timed at 22 miles per hour (35 kph) over short distances. That's almost as fast as a man can run.

Reptile Word Search

See if you can solve this reptile word search. All of the words listed below can be found by reading either forward, backward, or diagonally. When you find a word, circle it on the grid and cross it off the list.

S	G	G	E	I	L	L	K	Z	B	T	E
A	L	L	I	G	A	T	O	R	S	W	G
E	P	G	T	U	R	T	L	E	O	B	A
S	K	U	C	A	K	M	R	S	L	P	L
L	K	B	A	N	J	O	H	I	S	S	F
E	V	I	R	A	F	U	H	O	D	H	U
T	Y	F	N	N	Q	W	V	T	C	P	O
A	S	O	I	G	G	M	I	R	J	Y	M
R	H	A	V	I	P	E	R	O	T	T	A
G	R	X	O	K	C	E	G	T	X	H	C
I	L	A	R	E	P	T	I	L	E	O	A
M	J	O	E	B	C	G	F	U	M	N	O

alligators	gecko	python	skin
camouflage	hiss	rain forest	tortoise
carnivore	iguana	reptile	turtle
eggs	migrate	sea	viper

Letter Ladder

Use the clues below to fill in the boxes. If you've answered correctly, the shaded squares will spell out a type of snake.

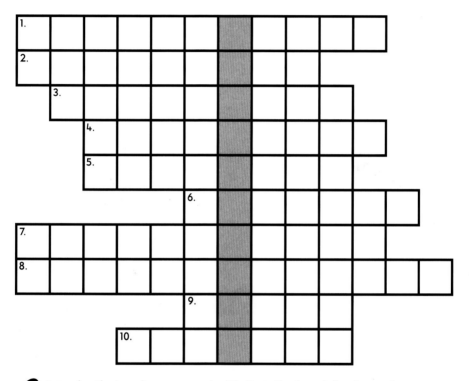

1. A snake that makes a sound with its tail when it is alarmed.
2. Any baby reptile that has just hatched from an egg.
3. A fierce reptile with a narrow head and V-shaped snout.
4. A reptile that changes color to fit its mood or surroundings.
5. A lizard with no legs.
6. The largest group of reptiles.
7. A deadly lizard that lives in the deserts of North America.
8. A reptile that opens a fan-like collar to scare off enemies.
9. A lizard with tiny hairs on the soles of its feet. It's a good climber.
10. A fish-eating crocodilian with spiky teeth.

True or False?

Which of these facts are true and which are false?
If you have read this book carefully, you will know the answers!

❶ All reptiles are predators and only eat meat.

❷ A scientist who studies reptiles is called a herpetologist.

❸ Many reptile species live near the icy poles.

❹ Marine iguanas are a kind of crocodile.

❺ Reptiles are cold-blooded and rely on the sun for warmth.

❻ The Komodo dragon is the world's smallest lizard.

❼ Snakes can find food by tasting the air with their tongues.

❽ All snakes have teeth that pump venom into their prey.

❾ You can tell crocodiles and alligators apart by looking at their teeth.

❿ A glass snake can snap off its tail to escape from predators.

⓫ Sea turtles hide their heads inside their shells for protection.

⓬ All reptiles lay eggs.

⓭ The tuatara has hardly changed since the time of the dinosaurs.

14 Chameleons can change their skin color to match their surroundings.

15 As they grow, snakes have to shed their skin from time to time.

16 Lizards are the slowest-moving reptiles.

17 Reptiles cannot chew their food. They tear it or swallow it whole.

18 All reptiles have four legs.

19 Snakes that squeeze their prey to death are called constrictors.

20 Caimans are bigger than crocodiles.

21 There are more crocodilians than any other kind of reptile.

22 Sea turtles lay their eggs in the sea.

23 The desert horned lizard squirts blood from its eyes to scare away enemies.

24 The largest tortoise in the world is the Kalahari tent tortoise.

25 Dinosaurs were reptiles.

26 Many snakes can climb trees.

27 There are reptiles on all the continents of the world.

28 The world's smallest reptile is a gecko.

ANSWERS: 1. False 2. True 3. False 4. False 5. True 6. False 7. False 8. False 9. True 10. True 11. False 12. False 13. True 14. True 15. True 16. False 17. True 18. False 19. True 20. False 21. False 22. False 23. True 24. False 25. True 26. True 27. False 28. True.

Glossary

adapt: to change slowly, over millions of years and many generations, to increase the chances for survival

camouflaged: having markings or coloring that help to blend in with one's surroundings. A well-camouflaged animal can hide from predators.

carnivore: an animal that eats meat

carrion: the flesh of dead animals

climate: the pattern of weather in a particular area of the world

cold-blooded: having a body temperature that changes according to the temperature of the surrounding air

constriction: killing a victim by squeezing until it can no longer breathe. This method is used by some snakes, including the boa and the anaconda.

digest: to break down food inside the body so that the nutrients and energy can be used by the body to grow and move

habitat: the place where an animal or plant lives. A habitat provides the right conditions for a species to survive.

hatchling: a baby reptile that has just hatched from an egg

heat sensors: special organs, located on an animal's head, that are sensitive to warmth. These sensors can help the animal know if there is another animal nearby.

herpetologist: a scientist who studies reptiles

hibernation: a deep sleep that lasts all winter. Going into hibernation helps animals to survive during cold months when there is little food available.

migrate: to travel from one place to another at a certain time of year, in search of food, mates, or nesting sites

oviparous: able to lay eggs

paralyze: to make another animal helpless and unable to move

poles: cold areas at the far north and south of the world that are covered in snow or ice all year round

predator: an animal that hunts and kills other animals for food

prey: an animal that is hunted and eaten by other animals

rain forest: an area covered thickly with plants and tall trees that receives rain almost every day. Steamy tropical rain forests are found near Earth's equator.

scutes: tough plates or scales that join together to make the protective, bony covering of crocodilians, turtles, and tortoises

slough: to shed the outer layer of skin. Reptiles do this regularly as they grow.

species: a group of animals or plants with similar characteristics whose members are are able to produce offspring together

swamp: an area of permanently wet, marshy ground

territory: an area where an animal lives and finds food. It will defend this area against other animals.

tropical: relating to the hot, wet areas of the world located near the Earth's equator

venomous: having a poisonous bite

vertebrate: any animal that has a backbone

vibrations: shaking movements that can be felt through the ground or air

viviparous: able to give birth to live young

Running your INTERFACT disk

Your INTERFACT CD-ROM will run on both PCs with Windows and on Apple Macs. To make sure that your computer meets the system requirements, check the list below.

MINIMUM SYSTEM REQUIREMENTS

PC
Processor: Pentium II (333MHz) or higher
Operating system: 95, 98, ME, 2000 or XP
Monitor: SVGA True Color
Screen resolution: 640 x 480 pixels
Graphics card: 4MB (or higher)
Soundcard: SoundBlaster compatible
Memory: 32 MB RAM
CD-ROM drive: four-speed
Internet browser: version 4 (or higher)
Headphones or speakers

APPLE MACINTOSH
Processor: 200MHz Power Mac, G3 or iMac
Operating system: 8.1—10.x (OS X)
Monitor: Millions of Colors
Screen resolution: 640 x 480 pixels
Graphics card: 4 MB (or higher)
Memory: 32 MB RAM
CD-ROM drive: four-speed
Internet browser: version 4.5 (or higher)
Headphones or speakers

Loading Your INTERFACT Disk

INTERFACT is easy to load. You can run INTERFACT from the CD-ROM—you don't need to install it on your hard drive. But, before you begin, quickly run through the checklist below to ensure that your computer is ready to run the program.

PC WITH WINDOWS

The program should start automatically when you put the disk in the CD-ROM drive. If it does not, follow these instructions.

1. Put the disk in the CD-ROM drive
2. Double-click on MY COMPUTER
3. Double-click on CD-ROM drive icon
4. Double-click on the REPTILES icon

APPLE MACINTOSH

1. Put the disk in the CD-ROM drive
2. Double-click on the INTERFACT icon
3. Double-click on the REPTILES icon

CHECKLIST

● First, make sure that your computer and monitor meet the system requirements listed on page 40.

● Check that your computer, monitor, and CD-ROM drive are all switched on and working normally.

● Close any other applications, such as word processors, that you have running.

● Switch off any screen savers that are running on your computer.

How to Use INTERFACT

INTERFACT is easy to use.
Now that you know how to load the
program (see page 41), read these simple
instructions and dive in!

There are five different and exciting features on the disk. Use the two alligator arrow keys on the right-hand side of the screen to click through the features. Each time you click, you'll see a preview of that feature. Click on the game icon at the top to make a selection.

For example, this is what your screen will look like when you play SNAKE ESCAPE, a game where you guess letters to spell out the name of a reptile. Once you've selected a feature, click on the main screen to start. Have fun!

K_m_d_ d_ag_n

LETTERS USED
e f t s i
b h

VOICE ON

Guess
the
reptile!

Click here when you see the feature you want to play.

Click on the arrow keys to scroll through the different features on the disk or to find your way to the exit.

Click on the VOICE ON button to hear the text read aloud.

main screen

VIDEO AND INTERNET

On the disk, you can watch video clips and follow links to reptile web sites. There are on-screen instructions that explain how to play the videos and log on to the Internet. Always ask permission before you go online, and read all the safe surfing tips.

DISK LINKS AND BOOKMARKS

As you read, watch for links like the one below. The orange boxes will direct you to an activity or video clip on the disk that relates to the page you are reading.

DISK LINK
Play SNAKE ESCAPE and guess reptile words to help the sea snake escape from the shark.

As you explore the disk, you'll bump into Bookmarks. These helpful links show you where to turn in the book for more information about the topic on the screen.

23

ACTIVITIES

Look for the activities on pages 34 to 37. You'll find a word search, a tricky letter ladder, and a true-or-false quiz to test your knowledge of reptiles.

HOT DISK TIPS

● If you need help finding your way around the disk, click the arrow keys to bring up the HELP icon. Click on the icon to go to the HELP section.

help icon   left arrow   right arrow

● Words that appear in a different color and are underlined are "hot." Touch them with the cursor for more information or an explanation of the word.

● When the cursor changes from an arrow ↑ to a hand 🖑 click your mouse and something will happen.

Troubleshooting

If you have a problem with your INTERFACT disk, you should find the solution here. If you still have a problem, then send us an e-mail at helpline@two-canpublishing.com.

Your Computer Setup

RESETTING SCREEN RESOLUTION

Resetting screen resolution in Windows 95, 98, Me, 2000, or XP:
Click on START at the bottom left of your screen, then click on SETTINGS, then CONTROL PANEL, then double-click on DISPLAY. Click on the SETTINGS tab at the top. Reset the Desktop area (or Display area) to 640 x 480 pixels and choose either 24-bit or True Color, then click APPLY. You may then need to restart your computer.

Resetting screen resolution for Apple Macintosh:
Click on the Apple symbol at the top left of your screen to access APPLE MENU ITEMS. Select CONTROL PANELS, then MONITORS (or MONITORS AND SOUND) then set the resolution to 640 x 480 and choose Millions of Colors. Screen resolutions can also be reset by clicking on the checkerboard symbol on the control strip.

ADJUSTING VIRTUAL MEMORY

Adjusting the Virtual Memory in Windows 95, 98, Me, 2000, or XP:
We do not recommend adjusting these settings, as Windows will automatically configure your system as required.

Adjusting the Virtual Memory on Apple Macintosh:
If you have 32 MB of RAM or more, REPTILES will run faster. If you do not have this amount of RAM free, hard disk memory can be used by switching on VIRTUAL MEMORY. Select the APPLE MENU, CONTROL PANELS, then select MEMORY. Switch on Virtual Memory. Set the amount of memory you require, then restart your machine.

Common Problems

 Disk will not run
There is not enough memory available. Quit all other applications and programs. If this does not work, increase your machine's RAM by adjusting the Virtual Memory (see left).

 There is no sound
Try each of the following:

1 Make sure that your speakers or headphones are connected to the speaker outlet at the back of your computer. They should NOT be plugged into the audio socket next to the CD-ROM drive at the front of the computer.

2 Make sure that the volume control is turned up, both on your external speakers and in the internal volume control.

3 (PCs only) Verify that your sound card is SoundBlaster compatible. To make your settings SoundBlaster compatible, see your sound card manual for more information.

 Graphics do not load or are of poor quality
Not enough memory is available, or you have the wrong display setting. Quit all other applications and programs and make sure that your monitor control is set to 24-bit or True Color.

 Graphics freeze or text boxes appear blank (Windows 95 or 98 only)
Graphics card acceleration is too high. Right-click your mouse on MY COMPUTER. Click on PROPERTIES, then PERFORMANCE, then GRAPHICS. Reset the hardware acceleration slider to NONE. Click OK. Restart your computer.

 Your machine freezes
There is not enough memory available. Either quit other applications and programs or increase your machine's RAM by adjusting the Virtual Memory (see left).

If you continue to have problems, check the ReadMe file on your Interfact disk for more information or contact your computer supplier.

Index